Mind the Gap:

Navigating and Maintaining
Relationships After Transformative
Healing

Written by Aubrey Perin

Mind the Gap: Navigating and Maintaining
Relationships After Transformative Healing
Written by Aubrey Perin

Cover and interior design by Aubrey Perin
ISBN: 979-8-9988227-7-3
First edition: 2025

For permissions or inquiries, contact:
Aubrey.i.perin@gmail.com

Printed in the United States of America

Contents

Dedication

This book is for everyone who has played a role
in my life, thank you.

Introduction — So You've Arrived

Healing changes everything — but not always in the ways you expect.

You may have thought the hard part was surviving the past. And it was. But there's a quiet new challenge that healing brings: learning how to live inside a life that was built by someone you no longer are.

You may feel distant from old friends, uneasy in familiar spaces, or uncertain about relationships that once felt essential.
You may even feel guilty for needing more space, more silence, more care for yourself.
This is not selfishness.
This is not abandonment.
This is healing doing its deeper work.

The voices of the past — the ones that tell you you're responsible for everyone else's comfort, that your worth depends on your compliance, that love requires sacrifice — may grow louder for a time.
Not because they are true, but because you are finally in a position to leave them behind.

Healing does not erase the good that once existed.
You are allowed to love your memories, to cherish the moments that made you who you are.

But you are not required to return to the patterns that once cost you your peace.
Growth will sometimes feel like grief.
Healing will sometimes feel like disloyalty.

You are not doing this wrong.
You are building a life that can hold the truth of who you are now.

There will be space between you and the people, places, and habits that shaped your unhealed life.
This space can feel painful. It can feel lonely. It can feel like a mistake.
It isn't.

That space — that gap — is the first true boundary your healing built.
Without it, you would bleed back into old dynamics and lose the coherence you fought so hard to find.

The gap is not the end of connection.
It's the beginning of real, healthy relationship — with yourself, and with others who are willing to meet you as you are, not as you were.

This book is not about labeling people as toxic or cutting yourself off from the world.
It's about recognizing the real, natural spaces that healing creates — and learning how to live inside them without collapsing, without shame, and without apology.

You are allowed to protect your peace.
You are allowed to stay whole.

The gap is sacred.
The work ahead is to carry it, honor it, and trust
that the space it creates is not emptiness — it is
breathing room for everything new you are
becoming.

Chapter 1: Recognizing the Gap: Healing Breaks the Old Patterns

You may not have noticed it at first.

Sometimes, the shift happens quietly: a conversation that feels different, a gathering that leaves you tired instead of connected, a sudden heaviness around people you once leaned on without question.
You realize, almost reluctantly, that something has changed.

Healing rearranges your internal landscape.
It alters what you need, what you can sustain, what you can offer.
It doesn't erase your love for others, but it changes the terms of your belonging.
You can no longer contort yourself to fit where you once felt at home.

This is the gap.
It isn't a judgment. It isn't proof that you've failed to heal.
It's the natural outcome of becoming someone who no longer needs to survive by shrinking, hiding, or absorbing what others cannot carry themselves.

The gap shows up first as dissonance:

- Feeling lonely in familiar company.

- Feeling drained after conversations that used to fill you up.

- Feeling unseen even while being praised for who you used to be.

At first, the gap feels wrong.
You may find yourself trying to close it, to lean harder into old roles, to shrink the discomfort by pretending nothing has changed.
This is a tender instinct — but it's a survival instinct, not a healing one.

Healing doesn't demand that you cut others off.
It asks that you **tell the truth** about where you are now.
It asks that you notice when closeness costs you your clarity.
It asks that you honor the gap not as a punishment, but as a necessary space where your new self can breathe.

You are not doing harm by changing.
You are not betraying anyone by needing space.
You are not ungrateful for loving yourself enough to stay whole.

The gap is your first invitation to build a new life — one that can hold both your history and your healing without requiring you to sacrifice either.

You don't have to rush to fix the space you now feel.
You don't have to fill it, deny it, or explain it away.
You only have to recognize it for what it is:

Proof that you are growing beyond what survival once demanded of you.

Why the Gap Exists

Healing does not simply mend old wounds. It changes the way you exist in relationships. The patterns that once defined how you showed up — patterns shaped by survival, fear, or a need to belong — begin to shift. Where you once stayed quiet to avoid conflict, you now feel the impulse to speak. Where you once absorbed the emotions of others to keep the peace, you now recognize the cost of carrying what is not yours. Healing alters what you can sustain, what you are willing to offer, and what you require in return.

Many relationships from your unhealed life were built on the foundation of these survival patterns. They were not necessarily unhealthy in every way, nor were they always consciously exploitative. But they were formed around who you needed to be at that time: adaptable, accommodating, sometimes invisible. As healing deepens, you begin to realize that relationships anchored in those old dynamics no longer fit as easily. The familiarity remains, but the comfort does not.

The gap you now feel between yourself and others is not evidence of failure. It is the natural distance that forms when growth demands new terms of engagement. Where you once maintained closeness by sacrificing authenticity, you now require mutual respect, shared accountability, and space for your full self to exist. Not every relationship will be able to adapt to these new terms, and that reality can be painful to confront.

It is important to understand that this gap is not punishment for anyone involved. It is not an indictment of those you have loved, nor a rejection of the history you share. Rather, it is a necessary space created by your healing — a space that allows you to maintain your integrity rather than regress into old, harmful patterns.

Some people may misunderstand your distance. They may experience it as abandonment, selfishness, or ingratitude. Their discomfort is real, but it is not yours to fix. Your responsibility is not to reassure others at the expense of your own coherence. Your responsibility is to stay true to the person you are becoming, even if it means allowing space to exist where there once was none.

Recognizing why the gap exists — and that it exists as a result of your growth, not your failure — is essential to navigating this stage of healing. It will help you resist the temptation to collapse the space out of guilt, nostalgia, or misplaced loyalty. It will give you permission to honor the work you have done and to protect the wholeness you are building.

What the Gap Feels Like

The experience of the gap is rarely loud or dramatic. More often, it reveals itself through subtle, persistent discomfort that can be difficult to explain even to yourself. Relationships that once felt effortless now feel strained. Conversations that once energized you now leave you feeling drained or unseen. Familiar routines no longer provide the same sense of belonging they once did.

Emotionally, the gap can provoke a wide range of reactions. It is common to feel guilt, especially toward people who were important to you before your healing process began. You may worry that by needing distance, you are betraying them or diminishing the love you once shared. Nostalgia can also be strong, pulling you back toward memories of connection and comfort, tempting you to overlook the very real ways in which those connections were maintained at the expense of your well-being.

Alongside guilt and nostalgia, doubt often creeps in. Healing is not a linear or constantly affirming experience, and the emergence of space between you and your old life can feel disorienting. You may question whether your growth is real or whether you are simply being selfish, cold, or overly critical. You may wonder if the peace you now seek is worth the relational tension it seems to create.

There are also physical and emotional cues that signal the presence of the gap. After spending time with certain people or in certain environments, you may feel exhaustion, emotional flatness, or even resentment. You may notice that you are holding your breath, tightening your body, or monitoring your words and reactions more carefully than you do with people who meet you in your healed state. These bodily signals are not betrayals; they are evidence that your system is recognizing where it no longer feels fully safe or seen.

At its core, the gap feels like a subtle mismatch between your internal reality and the external dynamics that once defined your relationships. It is not that you have stopped loving or caring for others; rather, you have stopped abandoning yourself to maintain proximity. This change creates friction, not because love has disappeared, but because the conditions required for love to be sustainable have shifted.

Recognizing the emotional and physical signs of the gap is an important part of protecting your healing. It allows you to move from confusion to clarity, from self-blame to self-respect. You are not imagining the distance. You are not manufacturing conflict. You are encountering, often for the first time, the truth of what it feels like to exist fully within yourself, even when the world around you has not shifted to meet you there.

Common Instincts to Collapse the Gap

When the gap between your healing and your old relationships becomes apparent, it is natural to want to close it. Most people do not experience the appearance of distance with indifference. They feel it acutely — often as anxiety, guilt, or grief. And because of that discomfort, many instinctively try to collapse the gap before fully understanding why it is there.

One of the most common instincts is to return to old patterns of people-pleasing. You may find yourself minimizing your needs, softening your boundaries, or silencing your discomfort to restore a sense of ease. Even as you recognize the cost of these behaviors, the familiar reward of temporary belonging can be powerfully tempting. When the people around you are accustomed to a version of you that met their needs without friction, reverting to that role can feel like a quick solution to the emotional tension the gap creates.

Another common instinct is rationalization. It is easy to downplay the emotional or relational shifts you are experiencing. You may tell yourself that you are overreacting, being too sensitive, or expecting too much. You may reframe unhealthy dynamics as normal, especially if they are deeply rooted in family systems, long-term friendships, or cultural expectations. Rationalization serves to relieve the discomfort of change by pretending that nothing important has really shifted — but it comes at the cost of your growing self-trust.

There is also the powerful instinct to absorb responsibility for other people's emotions. When you notice that someone is hurt, confused, or frustrated by your new boundaries or distance, you may feel compelled to fix their feelings. You may interpret their pain as evidence that you are doing something wrong, rather than as a natural response to change. This can lead to unnecessary apologies, unearned guilt, and the abandonment of the space your healing requires.

It is important to recognize these instincts not as failures, but as the remnants of survival strategies that once served you well. People-pleasing, rationalizing, and over-responsibility were ways of protecting yourself, maintaining connection, and securing safety in environments where your full authenticity may not have been welcomed or supported.

Now, however, these strategies can work against your healing. Attempting to collapse the gap may bring short-term relief, but it ultimately risks undermining the work you have done to become whole. Closing the space prematurely invites old patterns to reassert themselves and makes it harder to sustain the growth you have fought for.

Honoring the gap requires resisting the urge to explain it away, diminish its reality, or repair the discomfort it causes in others at your own expense. It requires patience — with yourself and with those around you — as you learn to stay steady inside the discomfort that growth naturally brings. Your task is not to eliminate the distance, but to understand it, respect it, and allow it to shape the next stage of your relational life with integrity.

Honoring your growth does not mean demanding that others honor it too. Growth is not measured by how well the people around you adjust to your changes. It is measured by your ability to stay present with your own discomfort without collapsing into old patterns. Healing asks you to trust that others are capable of managing their own feelings, just as you are learning to manage yours.

Setting boundaries, recognizing distance, and navigating change are acts of self-respect — not declarations of superiority. The work is to remain steady, compassionate, and clear, without using your growth as a weapon or expecting others to understand what they may not yet be ready to see. True healing makes space for your humanity *and* theirs.

The Gap Is Not Punishment — It's Protection

It is easy to mistake the discomfort of the gap for a sign that something has gone wrong. In the absence of familiar closeness, you may wonder if you are isolating yourself unnecessarily or hurting others by changing. The pain of distance can feel like punishment — for you, for the people who love you, or for the history you shared together. But the truth is simpler and kinder: the gap is not punishment. It is protection.

Healing does not remove your capacity for love. It clarifies the conditions under which love can exist without self-betrayal. Before healing, you may have mistaken proximity for connection, compliance for loyalty, or emotional labor for intimacy. Growth demands that these distortions fall away, and with their departure, space naturally opens between you and the relationships or environments that depended on them.

The gap protects your new alignment. It gives you room to recognize when old dynamics try to reassert themselves and to choose a different response. Without this space, the gravitational pull of old survival strategies would be overwhelming. Without this breathing room, it would be far too easy to slide back into patterns that feel familiar but cost you your coherence.

A note about coherence:
Healing is not just about feeling better; it is about becoming more fully yourself. Coherence means that your internal experiences — your emotions, values, needs, and actions — begin to align instead of pulling you in conflicting directions. When you are coherent, you do not have to betray your inner truth to maintain your relationships or your sense of safety. Protecting coherence is the heart of healing. It allows you to move through the world with

integrity, clarity, and self-respect, even when old patterns try to pull you back into familiar, but harmful, roles.

Protection does not always feel good in the moment. It often feels lonely, disorienting, and even cruel. But it is only by honoring the gap — by allowing the space between your healing and the unhealed systems around you to exist — that you create the possibility for authentic connection to emerge over time. Rushing to close the distance would not restore what was lost. It would simply recreate the conditions that required you to abandon yourself in the first place.

The relationships that can survive and thrive in the presence of the gap are the ones that can evolve alongside you. They are built not on the performance of closeness, but on mutual respect, honesty, and the willingness to navigate discomfort together. Some connections will adapt. Others will fall away. Both outcomes are acts of truth, not failures of love.

Honoring the gap does not mean walling yourself off from others. It means choosing to engage from a place of wholeness rather than from fear, obligation, or the need to maintain a version of yourself that no longer exists. It means trusting that space, when held with care and integrity, does not destroy relationships — it refines them.

The gap is not the absence of connection. It is the environment where real, sustainable connection is allowed to grow.

Chapter 2: The Call to Return: How Old Voices Pull You Back

Healing often begins quietly. So does the pressure to abandon it.

Once you have created space between your old patterns and your emerging self, it does not take long for familiar forces to try to fill that space. Some of these forces are external — people who expect you to return to roles you no longer fit. Others are internal — emotions and instincts formed long ago that still believe your survival depends on belonging at any cost.

The call to return is not always loud or obvious. It often comes dressed in the language of love, loyalty, or responsibility. It tells you that change is abandonment, that growth is selfishness, that distance is cruelty. It urges you to soften your boundaries, to doubt your needs, to make yourself smaller in order to preserve the comfort of others.

Understanding this call — and learning to hear it without obeying it — is essential to maintaining your coherence.

You do not have to hate the people who pull at you. You do not have to deny the love you have for them or the gratitude you feel for what you once shared. But you do have to recognize when the love

they offer, or the love you feel, is being used —
knowingly or not — to draw you back into old
patterns that no longer serve your healing.

The goal of this chapter is not to harden you. It is
not to teach you to view others as threats or
enemies. It is to offer you clarity: a way to stay
compassionate without collapsing, to stay present
without abandoning yourself, to stay loving without
surrendering your growth.

The call to return is real. It is powerful.
But so is your ability to recognize it — and to
choose differently.

Emotional Flashbacks: How They Disguise Themselves as Loyalty

Emotional flashbacks are not always dramatic or
recognizable at first. They often arrive quietly, not
as vivid memories, but as sudden floods of feeling:
guilt, fear, panic, obligation. You may find yourself
overwhelmed by a sense that you are doing
something wrong simply by holding your ground,
setting a boundary, or choosing space. These
emotions can feel so urgent and convincing that it
becomes difficult to separate your present reality
from the emotional survival patterns of your past.

Unlike memories that recall specific events,
emotional flashbacks trigger the body and mind into
reliving the *state* of being trapped, small, or unsafe.
You may not remember exactly when you learned
that being loved required you to be accommodating,

compliant, or invisible — but the feeling returns as if no time has passed. This is why the call to return to old dynamics can feel not just familiar, but necessary, even when you know intellectually that your healing demands something different.

One of the most deceptive qualities of emotional flashbacks is that they often disguise themselves as loyalty. You may feel that honoring your relationships means sacrificing your boundaries, silencing your needs, or shrinking back into old roles. You may convince yourself that healing is selfish, that stability is betrayal, or that your discomfort is proof you are abandoning the people you love.

In truth, loyalty built on self-abandonment is not loyalty at all — it is survival. And healing is not betrayal — it is a return to integrity.

Recognizing emotional flashbacks for what they are is not about blaming yourself for feeling them. It is about creating enough space inside yourself to question whether the emotional urgency you feel matches the reality you are living now. Not every pang of guilt, fear, or sadness is a sign that you are doing something wrong. Sometimes it is a sign that you are doing something brave.

Healing asks you to pause when the old feelings surge up and ask different questions:

"Is this truly about today, or is it the past trying to reclaim me?"

"Am I responding to the person in front of me, or to someone from my past who once needed me to disappear?"

"Is the fear I feel today based on the risks of now, or the risks I survived before?"

"Am I shrinking because the situation demands it, or because I have been taught to survive that way?"

"Does honoring myself today truly harm anyone, or does it simply change what they expect from me?"

Not every strong feeling is a truth you must obey. Sometimes, it is an old echo — and your work is to hear it without reenacting it.

Guilt, Obligation, and Shame: The Old Tools to Maintain Old Dynamics

Even after recognizing emotional flashbacks, the specific emotions they trigger can still be powerful enough to challenge your clarity. Guilt, obligation, and shame are often the first tools used — consciously or unconsciously — to pull you back toward old relational patterns. They can feel righteous, familiar, and urgent, making it difficult to recognize when they are serving a dynamic you no longer wish to sustain.

Guilt emerges when you begin to prioritize your needs and boundaries over others' expectations. It tells you that by choosing yourself, you are hurting someone else. It frames self-respect as harm, and self-protection as betrayal. Guilt is persuasive because it appeals to your care for others, weaponizing your empathy against your own healing. It insists that if someone else is uncomfortable or hurt, you must be at fault — regardless of the health or necessity of the boundary you have set.

Obligation follows close behind. Obligation reminds you of everything you have been given, everything you owe, every bond that once kept you tethered to the people and systems around you. It insists that growth is abandonment, that loyalty requires self-sacrifice, that love demands compliance. Obligation is especially difficult to navigate when it ties itself to family roles, long-standing friendships, or cultural expectations that frame endurance and accommodation as virtues.

Shame, the most corrosive of the three, tells you that it is not just your actions that are wrong — it is your very being. Shame convinces you that your healing is selfish, that your new boundaries are evidence of a cold heart or a fractured loyalty. It clouds your ability to recognize that what you are building — integrity, self-trust, coherence — is not a betrayal of love but a fuller expression of it.

These emotions are not inherently wrong or bad. Guilt, obligation, and shame often originate from places of deep relational intelligence — the desire to belong, to honor connection, to act with care. But when they are used to preserve dynamics that require you to abandon yourself, they become obstacles to your healing rather than evidence of your goodness.

Recognizing these emotions for what they are allows you to pause, reflect, and choose your response with intention. Feeling guilty does not necessarily mean you have done something wrong. Feeling obligated does not mean you must comply. Feeling ashamed does not mean you are broken. These feelings are signals to be explored, not commands to be obeyed.

A reminder about the gap:
When strong emotions surge — especially guilt, obligation, or shame — it can feel as if you must act immediately to restore comfort or repair connection. This sense of urgency is often a sign that old patterns are trying to reassert themselves. In these moments, honoring the gap becomes even more important.

The gap gives you permission to pause. It creates a space where you can sit with your feelings without being forced to react to them. Choosing not to act immediately is not abandonment, selfishness, or failure. It is a way of protecting your coherence while you discern whether the action you are being pulled toward truly serves your healing — or only serves to maintain a pattern you have outgrown.

As you move through healing, your work is not to eliminate guilt, obligation, or shame entirely. It is to learn when these emotions are aligned with your integrity — and when they are echoes of a past that no longer defines you.

A note about material obligations:
Throughout this book, when we speak of obligation, we are referring to emotional and relational indebtedness — the internalized belief that your value depends on maintaining certain roles, dynamics, or patterns. We are not referring to legal, financial, or material obligations, which carry different responsibilities and should be addressed separately.

In rare but serious cases, healing may reveal that material exploitation — financial abuse, coerced agreements, or fraud — occurred during a time when your unhealed patterns made you vulnerable. If you believe you are entangled in such a situation, it is important to seek qualified legal counsel. This book will not attempt to provide legal advice, but your healing journey may rightfully include untangling those forms of harm through professional support.

Emotional healing is vital, but it does not replace the need for legal protections when material rights have been violated.

Recognizing Manipulation Without Vilifying People You Love

As you begin to hold firmer boundaries and stay rooted in your healing, you may start to notice behaviors from others that feel uncomfortable or coercive. You may recognize moments when conversations, emotions, or dynamics seem designed — consciously or unconsciously — to pull you back into old patterns. This is often the first painful glimpse of manipulation.

The word "manipulation" carries heavy weight. It is often associated with malice, cruelty, or deliberate harm. But in many cases, manipulation within personal relationships is not driven by conscious malice. It is a survival tactic — a way that unhealed people attempt to maintain connection, control, or emotional regulation using the tools they know. Recognizing manipulation does not require you to demonize the people you love. It requires you to see the patterns clearly enough to protect your healing without collapsing into blame or resentment.

Manipulation can take many forms:

- Guilt-tripping ("After everything I've done for you…")

- Gaslighting ("You're being dramatic; that's not what happened.")

- Emotional withholding ("If you loved me, you wouldn't need space.")

- Conditional affection ("You're only good when you behave the way I expect.")

These behaviors often trigger strong emotional flashbacks, reigniting old feelings of fear, guilt, or shame. They create urgency to fix, appease, or prove yourself. They pull you toward abandoning your own clarity in order to restore a familiar — but costly — form of belonging.

Recognizing manipulation is not about becoming cynical or suspicious of everyone you love. It is about developing the capacity to hold two truths at once:

- Someone can love you *and* still attempt to pull you back into patterns that are no longer healthy.

- You can love someone *and* still refuse to participate in dynamics that require you to abandon yourself.

You are not disloyal for noticing when patterns are unhealthy. You are not cruel for refusing to reenact them. You are not judgmental for choosing distance when proximity requires your diminishment.

Learning to recognize manipulation without vilifying others protects your healing by allowing you to respond with clarity rather than anger. It allows you to move away from unhealthy dynamics without needing to create villains. It preserves your compassion — not by collapsing into old roles, but by staying true to yourself while still honoring the complexity of others.

Not everyone who manipulates you is trying to harm you. Many are trying to survive in ways they have never questioned. Your work is not to fix them. Your work is to protect the healing you have fought to claim — with kindness when possible, with distance when necessary, and always with integrity.

Compassionate Clarity: Loving Without Collapsing

Healing does not require you to stop loving the people who helped shape your life. It does not demand that you erase your past or harden your heart against those who cannot meet you in your new alignment. True healing asks something quieter and more difficult: that you learn to love without collapsing.

Compassionate clarity means being able to see people as they are, without needing to make them smaller or safer than they choose to be. It means recognizing their struggles, their limitations, and their wounds — and still choosing to protect the space your healing needs, even when that choice is uncomfortable.

Loving without collapsing begins with accepting that you are no longer available for certain patterns, even if you once endured them in the name of connection. You are no longer willing to shrink yourself to preserve someone else's comfort. You are no longer willing to silence your needs to avoid the discomfort of others. You are no longer willing to mistake compliance for love.

Compassionate clarity allows you to stay grounded when others pull at your old wounds. It reminds you that your healing is not a weapon to use against others, nor a wall to hide behind. It is simply the truth of who you are now — and it deserves to be honored without apology.

Holding compassionate clarity means allowing yourself to grieve what cannot be repaired, to bless what must be released, and to remain open to connection where mutual respect and authenticity can grow. It means you can say "I love you" — and still say "no." It means you can remember the good without recreating the harm. It means you can carry tenderness without carrying dysfunction.

Compassionate clarity is the bridge between your healing and the world. It allows you to engage with others not from fear or obligation, but from genuine choice. It protects your ability to love freely, without surrendering the coherence you have worked so hard to build.

You are allowed to love people who cannot meet you where you are.
You are allowed to love them — and still walk your own path.

Loving without collapsing is not coldness.
It is the warmth of a love rooted in truth rather than fear.

It is the final proof that your healing is not a rejection of love.
It is a return to it.

Imagine standing at the edge of a forest with someone you love deeply. You have spent years walking together through twisting trails, often carrying each other when the path grew too hard. But now, you can see that the trail ahead splits. One path asks you to shrink, to circle endlessly around old landmarks. The other leads forward into unknown terrain.

You turn to your companion and reach out, hoping they will walk beside you into this new place. Maybe they hesitate. Maybe they stay behind.

You can love them still. You can bless their journey, even if it takes them somewhere you cannot follow.

And it is okay to grieve — to feel the weight of that moment, the ache of distance between two hearts that once moved as one. Grief is not a sign you have failed. It is a sign that you have loved deeply, and that you are now loving yourself deeply enough to keep walking.

You can carry both love and grief as you turn toward the path that calls you — not because you

have stopped loving them, but because you have
finally started loving yourself enough to keep going.

Chapter 3: Mapping the Terrain: Types of Relationships You'll Encounter

Healing changes the way you move through the world. It doesn't just alter your internal landscape; it reshapes the way you experience connection, belonging, and relationship. This change can feel disorienting at first. The paths you once walked without question now ask for careful navigation. The bonds you once trusted to anchor you may begin to strain under the weight of your growth.

It is important to recognize that healing does not require severing every tie to your past. It does not demand that you view every unchanged relationship as a failure or threat. Healing asks for clarity, not cruelty. It asks you to see where relationships can adapt and deepen — and where they must be held more loosely, approached with different expectations, or, in some cases, gently released.

Mapping the terrain of your relationships after healing is an act of discernment, not judgment. It is the work of learning to trust your new coherence — to trust that the shifts you feel are not betrayals, but invitations to align your connections with your truer self.

A note on mapping:
When we speak of mapping your relationships, we are not suggesting that you must chart them formally or create a rigid plan for how each connection should unfold. Mapping, in this context, means allowing yourself to notice the natural shifts in how you feel, connect, and engage with others as your healing deepens. It is an organic process of discernment, not a directive to analyze or control your relationships.

That said, if you find it helpful to reflect on your connections more concretely — through journaling, diagramming, or quiet contemplation — you are welcome to do so. There is no one right way to honor the changes you are living through. Your awareness is the map. Your feelings are the guide.

Some friendships and relationships will grow with you.
Some will change shape.
Some will fall away.
And new ones, ones that meet you in your wholeness, will come.

You do not have to rush to categorize or decide everything at once. Healing is not a transaction; it is a living process.
But learning to recognize the different ways

relationships can evolve — or resist evolution — will help you move forward with greater compassion, patience, and self-respect.

In this chapter, we will explore the different types of relational shifts you are likely to encounter. We will not tell you who to keep or who to leave behind. Instead, we will offer a way of seeing — a compass rose, of sorts — to help you navigate the unfolding map of your new emotional reality with steadiness, dignity, and hope.

Friends Who Can Reorganize with You: Building Bridges, New Rhythms

Not every relationship from your past will fall away as you heal. Some friendships, often the ones built on mutual respect rather than survival patterns, have the capacity to reorganize alongside your growth. These are the relationships where change is not seen as a threat, but as an invitation — where the bond is strong enough to stretch, adjust, and find new rhythms without collapsing.

Friends who can reorganize with you may not fully understand every aspect of your healing. They may not know exactly what has shifted inside you or why you now move differently through the world. But what they offer is a willingness to meet you where you are, even when the landscape feels unfamiliar. They listen when you speak your needs. They respect your boundaries without punishment. They are willing to learn who you are becoming, not just cling to who you used to be.

Reorganization often happens gradually. It may begin with small adjustments: different ways of spending time together, different types of conversations, a different pace of closeness. Some friends will instinctively recognize and support your growth. Others may need time to adjust, to grieve the ways the relationship is changing, and to find their footing again. Patience, honesty, and flexibility are essential on both sides.

Building new rhythms with old friends requires communication. It asks for moments of vulnerability — sharing your needs and boundaries without demanding that others conform or fully understand. It asks for grace — allowing your friends the space to have their own reactions, their own journeys of adjustment. And it asks for discernment — recognizing when the reorganization is mutual and when it is being carried entirely by you.

A reorganized friendship does not always look the same as it once did. Some friends may become closer, finding deeper connection through the honesty that healing brings. Others may drift slightly, still present in your life but occupying a different emotional space. Both outcomes are valid. Both can be held with gratitude rather than resentment.

Trust that the friends who are capable of meeting you in your coherence will reveal themselves over time. Their presence will feel less like effort and more like ease — not because the relationship is without challenges, but because it no longer requires you to disappear to maintain it.

Healing does not always mean losing. Sometimes, it means rediscovering connection on new, sturdier ground.

Friends You Love But Must Love Differently: Releasing Expectations

Not every friendship that survives your healing will survive in the same form. Some friendships, even those built on genuine love and shared history, will require new boundaries, new expectations, and sometimes new distance. This is not a failure of love. It is a natural part of growing beyond the patterns that once shaped your relationships.

Loving differently begins with releasing the idea that love must look the way it always has. It requires you to recognize that emotional proximity — frequent conversations, deep involvement, unquestioned access — is not always the healthiest form of connection after healing. Sometimes, loving someone well means loving them with more space, fewer obligations, and greater respect for your own emotional capacity.

It is common to feel grief when you realize that a friendship can no longer sustain the same level of closeness. You may mourn the memories you shared, the ease you once felt, the versions of yourselves that fit together more easily. This grief is valid. It honors the real connection that existed, even as you honor the reality that continuing the relationship unchanged would require you to betray yourself.

Adjusting the terms of a friendship does not mean you must cut ties abruptly or treat the other person with coldness. Often, it means quietly shifting your expectations. You may become less available for emotional caretaking. You may choose to engage more intentionally and less frequently. You may find yourself appreciating the friend for who they are, rather than struggling with who they are not.

Releasing expectations allows you to preserve the essence of the relationship — the genuine care, the shared history, the affection — without demanding that it meet needs it can no longer fulfill. It frees you from cycles of disappointment and resentment. It lets you love without needing the relationship to prove itself by fitting your healing perfectly.

Some friendships will adapt to this quieter, more spacious form of love. Others may drift naturally over time. Some friends may sense the shift without fully understanding it, feeling the distance but not the rupture. This, too, can be held with grace.

A note on relationships and healing:
As you move deeper into healing, you may find that all relationships — even those with family members, including parents — begin to feel more like friendships than roles. Healing often dissolves the old hierarchies that once governed connection. Relationships built on authority, obligation, or unexamined expectation begin to shift toward relationships built on mutual respect, choice, and emotional reciprocity.

This does not mean there is a right or wrong way for a relationship to evolve. Some bonds may retain a sense of structure or tradition that feels meaningful to both people. Others may transition into quieter, more equal forms of friendship. Healing simply invites you to meet others — including family — not from a place of duty or survival, but from the place where authentic connection can grow.

You are allowed to continue loving people who no longer occupy the same space in your life.
You are allowed to bless what the friendship was — and what it still can be — without forcing it to be something it can no longer sustain.

Love does not always end because it changes. Sometimes, it endures precisely because you allowed it to evolve.

Family Systems That Resist Change: Setting Firm Yet Loving Limits

Family systems are often the most difficult relationships to navigate after healing. Unlike friendships, which are usually formed voluntarily, family ties are rooted in history, tradition, and shared identity. The roles assigned within family structures — caregiver, peacemaker, scapegoat, protector — often become deeply ingrained long before you are capable of questioning them. Healing challenges these roles, and in doing so, challenges the system itself.

When you begin to move differently — when you set boundaries, express needs, or step out of familiar roles — family systems often experience this change as a threat. Not necessarily because they wish you harm, but because systems resist change. Patterns that have endured for years, even generations, seek to maintain themselves. Your growth can feel like disruption to those who have benefited, consciously or unconsciously, from the old ways of relating.

Setting boundaries with family is not about rejecting your history. It is about protecting your future. It is about choosing not to sacrifice your coherence to maintain a pattern that demands your silence, compliance, or invisibility.

Boundaries do not mean you stop loving your family. They mean you stop allowing love to be defined by conditions that cost you your integrity.

Boundaries with family may take many forms:

- You may limit the topics you are willing to discuss.

- You may limit the amount of time you spend together.

- You may limit the emotional access others have to you — choosing to share only with those who can receive you with respect.

- In some cases, you may step away entirely, at least for a time, when the system proves unwilling or unable to honor your boundaries.

Loving boundaries are not punitive. They are not acts of vengeance or cruelty. Loving boundaries are acts of clarity. They recognize that love without respect is not sustainable. They honor both your healing and the humanity of those who may not yet be able to meet you in it.

You are allowed to want connection with your family. You are allowed to grieve when it cannot happen easily.
But you are not required to collapse yourself to earn their acceptance.

Healing may reveal painful truths: that some family members can adapt, and others cannot; that some bonds will strengthen, and others will fray. These truths are not indictments of your worth — or theirs. They are simply reflections of where others are in their own journeys — journeys you cannot control.

Boundaries allow you to continue loving with an open heart without abandoning yourself.
They allow you to bless and cherish what was good, mourn what was lost, and protect what you are building.

Family is not owed your healing.
But you are owed the freedom to live it.

Making New Friends: Trusting Your New Self to Choose Aligned Connections

One of the quieter griefs of healing is the feeling of loneliness it can create. As old patterns fall away and old dynamics shift, you may find yourself standing in a wide, unfamiliar space between the life you have outgrown and the life that has not yet fully arrived. This space can feel endless at times. It can tempt you to doubt whether deeper connection is possible outside the systems you once knew.

But healing does not end with loss. It clears space for something new — relationships built not on survival, performance, or inherited roles, but on mutual recognition and resonance.

Trusting yourself to make new connections after healing can feel daunting. Without old survival strategies to guide you — without the automatic pull toward fixing, pleasing, or enduring — you may wonder what healthy connection even looks like. You may fear choosing poorly, rushing into relationships that replay old patterns under new disguises.

This fear is natural. It deserves your patience, not your judgment.

Moving slowly is a form of wisdom, not failure. Pausing to listen to your intuition is an act of self-respect.
Trusting your own discomfort — the small hesitations, the subtle unease — is part of honoring the coherence you have built.

Aligned connections often feel different than what you have been conditioned to seek. They may feel quieter at first, less urgent – maybe even boring. There may be less immediate intensity, but more ease. Conversations may unfold naturally without a sense of performance or caretaking. Trust may build gradually, without drama or demand.

A note on stability and boredom:
If stability feels boring at first, it does not mean the connection is hollow or that something important is missing. It may simply mean your nervous system is adjusting to the absence of chaos, intensity, or

emotional urgency. When you have been conditioned to associate emotional highs and lows with love, steadiness can feel unfamiliar — even dull. This is not a flaw in the connection or in you. It is part of learning to trust a kind of safety that does not demand performance, rescue, or survival strategies. Over time, what once felt boring may begin to feel like peace — and peace, properly understood, is anything but empty.

You are allowed to take your time. You are allowed to let new people show you who they are through their consistency, their kindness, and their willingness to honor your boundaries. You are allowed to trust that your healed self will recognize resonance more clearly than your surviving self once could.

Not every new acquaintance will become a lasting connection. Some may pass through your life gently, offering a glimpse of kindness without the need for permanence. Others will root more deeply, becoming companions who meet you as you are, not as you perform.

The relationships that emerge from your coherence will not require you to abandon yourself.
They will not demand that you collapse your needs to maintain belonging.
They will allow you to stay whole — and to be loved as whole.

Feeling lonely after healing is not a punishment. It is a clearing. It is a necessary stillness where new, truer forms of connection can take root.

Trust yourself to recognize the people who will walk with you not because they need you to be anything other than who you are — but because they cherish the wholeness of who you have become.

Chapter 4: Boundaries: The Framework That Protects the New You

Healing transforms not just how you feel inside yourself, but how you move through the world.
It changes what you can offer — and what you can no longer offer without losing your integrity. It changes how you love, how you receive love, and what you recognize as sustainable connection.

But healing, by itself, is not self-sustaining. Without clear, living boundaries, even the strongest coherence can be pulled back into old patterns of survival. Without protection, your new self is vulnerable — not because it is weak, but because it is tender, unfamiliar, and still finding its footing.

Boundaries are not punishments. They are not walls of cruelty or acts of aggression.
They are frameworks of care — for yourself, for your relationships, and for the life you are building.

A healthy boundary is an act of respect:

- Respect for your own needs and values

- Respect for the emotional reality of others

- Respect for the relationship itself, by refusing to let it depend on the abandonment of your truest self

A note on unhealthy boundaries:

Not everything called a boundary is truly protective. Sometimes what is framed as a boundary is actually an attempt to control, punish, or withdraw from relational responsibility. Unhealthy boundaries often sound like ultimatums ("Do this, or you're cut off"), rigid walls ("I refuse to feel anything about this"), or silent demands that others change to preserve our comfort.

Healthy boundaries are anchored in your own behavior and choices — what you will or will not participate in — without requiring others to change in order for you to remain whole. Healthy boundaries also collaborate: they create space for the healthy boundaries of others to exist alongside your own. They build connection that honors mutual respect, emotional reality, and choice.

By contrast, unhealthy boundaries attempt to manage or shut down others' emotional experiences. They prioritize emotional avoidance over authentic connection. A boundary that silences someone else's healthy feelings, simply because they are uncomfortable to hear, is not protection — it is control.

Healing boundaries create freedom. Controlling boundaries create fear.

Learning the difference protects both your healing and your relationships.

Setting boundaries does not mean you are rejecting people.
It means you are refusing to sacrifice yourself in order to preserve illusions of safety, closeness, or obligation.
It means you are choosing connection that can survive honesty, rather than connection that demands performance.

Throughout this chapter, we will explore how to recognize when emotional labor is no longer yours to carry, how to say no without apology, and how to understand boundaries not as defensive walls, but as the container that protects the coherence you fought so hard to build.

You have done the work of healing.
You deserve to live inside that healing — protected, steady, and free.

Recognizing When You Are Doing Emotional Labor That Isn't Yours

Healing changes not only how you care for yourself, but how you recognize the care you extend to others. One of the most important — and often most difficult — lessons in maintaining coherence is learning when you are carrying emotional labor that was never yours to hold.

Emotional labor is the invisible work of managing feelings, smoothing tensions, anticipating needs, and absorbing discomfort — often without acknowledgment or reciprocation. It can look like always being the peacemaker, the translator, the caretaker, the one who "understands" even when others do not meet you with the same consideration.

In relationships rooted in old survival patterns, emotional labor often becomes invisible. It feels like love. It feels like loyalty. It feels like your natural role. Healing allows you to recognize when that labor is no longer about love, but about maintaining connection at the cost of your own emotional health.

Carrying emotional labor that isn't yours often feels like:

- Constantly monitoring someone else's mood and adjusting yourself to keep the peace

- Feeling responsible for fixing or managing other people's emotional reactions

- Silencing your needs to avoid burdening others

- Anticipating and accommodating unspoken expectations out of fear of conflict or disapproval

45

- Feeling guilt or anxiety when you prioritize your own boundaries or emotional truth

It is important to remember: empathy is not the same as enmeshment.
Compassion does not require self-abandonment.

When you find yourself carrying emotional labor that belongs to someone else, the work of healing is to notice it — without shame — and gently set it down. You are not obligated to carry what others refuse to tend to within themselves.

A note on relational communication:
When you notice yourself carrying emotional labor that is no longer yours, you are not required to silently set it down without conversation. Healing also creates space to name your patterns openly and invite relational clarity. You might say, "Right now, I feel like you expect me to help you manage your feelings. Is that correct?"

If you know that the expectation is there, you might say, "I understand that you want me to help you with how you feel. While I can see that you are hurt, frustrated, or angry, I can only validate your feelings. I am not willing to solve this for you."

This approach honors both your emotional truth and the possibility of continued connection, without collapsing into old survival roles.

When speaking to children, the tone must shift appropriately. Children do require emotional guidance, and your role includes helping them process safely. In those cases, you might say, "I understand that you are hurt, frustrated, or angry — and I know how incredibly scary that can feel. Would you like to talk about what's making you feel this way, or would you like me to just sit with you in these feelings for a little while first?"

Boundaries are not barriers to connection. They are invitations to healthier, more conscious connection — for yourself, and for those you love.

Recognizing misplaced emotional labor is not about becoming cold or detached. It is about restoring the balance of care: offering empathy without absorbing, offering presence without performance, offering love without sacrificing your coherence.

In healthy relationships, emotional labor flows both ways, chosen freely and carried willingly.
In unhealthy patterns, emotional labor becomes expectation — silent, endless, and assumed.

The first step in protecting your coherence is noticing when emotional care has stopped being mutual and has begun to require your disappearance.

A note on noticing:
Protecting your coherence does not require hypervigilance. You do not need to scan every interaction for signs of danger or betrayal. Healing invites a different kind of noticing — one rooted in attunement to yourself rather than constant monitoring of others.

When emotional care stops being mutual, you will not need to hunt for evidence. You will feel it: a subtle sense of imbalance, a tightening inside you, a quiet intuition that presence is costing you more than it should.

Noticing is not about suspicion. It is about trusting the wisdom of your own emotional experience — and responding with care when your coherence signals that something needs attention.

You are allowed to step out of emotional roles that once kept you connected to others at the cost of yourself.
You are allowed to let others carry their own growth, their own feelings, their own responsibilities.

Freedom begins not with abandoning empathy, but with refusing to mistake enmeshment for love.

Saying No Without Shame or Apology

Imagine standing in a familiar room with someone you care about.

They ask you for something — your time, your agreement, your silence, your caretaking.

You feel the old tug: the instinct to smile, to nod, to say yes before you've even heard yourself think.

The pressure to preserve connection at the cost of yourself rises, just as it always has.

But this time, something different happens.

You hear yourself say, simply:

"No."

No apology.
No elaborate justification.
No guilt trailing behind your voice, trying to make it softer or safer.

Just the word.
Clear.
Honest.
Whole.

The air shifts. Maybe it feels strange, or frightening, or powerful.

Maybe the other person blinks in surprise. Maybe they push. Maybe they don't.

But you do not collapse. The room is still standing. You and the person you're speaking with are both

still living.
You do not chase after the discomfort.

You remain standing inside your own coherence.
And for the first time, you realize: saying no did not
end you.
It protected you.

Learning to say no is one of the most profound acts
of self-respect that healing makes possible.
It is also one of the most difficult.

For many people, saying no has been tangled up
with guilt, shame, or fear.

- Guilt, because they were taught that saying
  no is selfish.

- Shame, because they were taught that saying
  no makes them cold or ungrateful.

- Fear, because they learned that saying no
  risks abandonment, rejection, or retaliation.

Healing separates your no from these old emotional
burdens. It reminds you that saying no is not an
attack. It is not a rejection of love. It is simply a way
of staying coherent — a way of honoring both
yourself and others by refusing to offer what you
cannot give freely.

A healthy no sounds like:

- "I'm not available for that."

- "I understand that's important to you, but I can't participate."

- "I care about you, and I need to honor my own limits right now."

- "I'm not able to carry that with you, but I respect that you're feeling a lot."

A note on boundaries and relational responsibility:

Saying no is a powerful act of coherence, but it is not an excuse to abandon relational care — especially in parent-child relationships or in settings where you hold legitimate responsibility for the wellbeing of others.

Some popular narratives about boundaries suggest that "no" must always be absolute, detached, or without emotional engagement. This misunderstanding can cause harm: it teaches avoidance rather than healthy containment.

When setting boundaries with children, for example, a healthy no looks different than it does with adults. It is not a withdrawal from the child's emotional experience. Instead, it offers clear, consistent limits while remaining present and connected. You might say:

- "I know you're used to this behavior, and I can't continue to model it. No, we are not getting another toy today."

- "I understand you want to stay up later, and I know how hard it is to stop having fun — but no, it's bedtime."

- "I see you're frustrated, and it's okay to feel that way. No, we're not having another sweet tonight."

Healthy boundaries respect both your coherence and the emotional development of those you are caring for.
Boundaries are not about cutting off.
They are about containing what needs care — including yourself, and including others — without collapsing or disappearing.

Notice that a healthy no does not require elaborate justification.
It does not come with endless explanations designed to soften the discomfort of others.
It stands quietly on its own — clear, kind, and unshakable.

Overexplaining your no often comes from a place of fear: the fear that others will not honor your boundaries unless you make yourself small enough, guilty enough, or pitiful enough to earn their acceptance. Healing asks you to give yourself a different kind of permission: the permission to set a boundary because you exist, not because you have exhausted yourself trying to deserve it.

You are allowed to say no simply because
something is not aligned with your needs, your
energy, or your truth.
You are allowed to say no without apology, without
guilt, and without losing your humanity.

A clean no respects others as much as it respects
yourself.
It trusts that healthy people will receive your no
without requiring you to sacrifice your coherence to
comfort them.

Learning to say no without shame is not about
becoming rigid or unkind.
It is about learning to trust that your boundaries are
worth honoring — even if they are misunderstood,
even if they are not celebrated, even if they are met
with discomfort.

Saying no is not closing your heart.
It is protecting the space where love, dignity, and
freedom can actually survive.

Boundaries Are the Container for the Coherence You Fought to Build

Healing is not simply a shift in feelings.
It is a shift in structure — an internal reorganization
of who you are allowed to be in relationship with
yourself and with others.
And every structure needs a container strong
enough to hold it.

Boundaries are that container.
They are not walls of fear. They are not weapons of isolation. They are the quiet, steady frameworks that allow your coherence to survive the friction of everyday life.

Without boundaries, even the most profound healing can slowly erode under the weight of external expectations, emotional entanglements, and internalized guilt.
Without boundaries, your coherence becomes something you visit in solitude but abandon in relationship.
Without boundaries, healing remains fragile — beautiful, but unsustained.

Boundaries do not make you rigid.
They make you real. And invite you to be real in all parts of your life.

A life without boundaries demands that you constantly shapeshift: adjusting to the needs, moods, and demands of others in order to preserve connection at any cost.
A life with boundaries allows you to stay whole: offering presence, love, and connection without losing the thread of who you are.

Boundaries are not punishments you impose on the world.
They are promises you make to yourself:

- I will not disappear to be loved.

- I will not betray myself to belong.

54

- I will not sacrifice my coherence to comfort those who cannot or will not meet me in it.

Living with boundaries means accepting that some people will misunderstand you.
It means grieving that some relationships cannot survive your refusal to collapse.
It means celebrating that the connections that do survive will be richer, deeper, and truer — not because you performed for them, but because you remained real within them.

The work of healing does not end with personal insight.
It matures into the daily practice of protecting the space where your new self can continue to grow.

Your coherence is sacred.
Your boundaries are the home where it lives.

Chapter 5: Staying Coherent

Living Inside Your Healing

Healing is not an event. It is not a single realization, a sudden arrival, or a permanent shield against pain. Healing is dynamic. It is a living relationship with yourself — one that requires tending, attention, and care.

Staying coherent does not mean staying rigid.
It does not mean holding yourself under constant scrutiny or policing your emotions for signs of "failure."
It means remaining in dialogue with yourself: noticing what strengthens you, what drains you, and what invites you to step away from your own wholeness.

Coherence is not something you achieve once and for all.
It is something you choose, day after day, moment after moment, especially when old patterns call you to disappear again.
It is something you protect — not through fear, but through presence.

Daily tending is not punishment.
It is the price and the privilege of building a life that feels like home inside your own body and mind.

Throughout this chapter, we will explore simple practices that help you stay coherent as you move through real life:

- Practices for noticing when you are carrying emotional weight that is not yours.

- Practices for learning to sit with yourself without shame or panic.

- Practices for following joy as a guide toward deeper alignment.

- Practices for loving what was good without collapsing back into what was harmful.

Healing does not require you to live perfectly.
It asks you to live attentively.
It asks you to stay awake to yourself, and to choose
— again and again — the life that grows from
coherence, not collapse.

You have already fought for your healing.
Now, you are learning how to live inside it.

Practices for Coherence

Healing invites you to build a daily relationship with
your coherence — not through rigid discipline, but
through steady, gentle tending.
These practices are not about control or self-
surveillance. They are about creating spaces in your
life where your wholeness can continue to breathe,
stretch, and grow.

You do not need to master every practice.
You do not need to perform healing perfectly.
You need only stay attentive to yourself —
returning again and again to what strengthens your
truth rather than eroding it.

Here are a few practices that can help you live inside your healing with grace and steadiness:

Emotional Audits: Whose Feelings Am I Carrying?

One of the first signs that coherence is slipping is the quiet weight of feelings that do not fully belong to you.
Without noticing, you may find yourself absorbing the guilt, fear, sadness, or frustration of others — carrying emotions that were never yours to resolve.

Practicing emotional audits helps you stay attuned to what is truly yours to hold.

A gentle audit might sound like:

- "Whose anger am I feeling right now?"

- "Is this sadness mine, or am I carrying it for someone else?"

- "Am I absorbing someone else's fear as my own?"

Emotional audits are not acts of blame or detachment.
They are acts of self-trust.
They allow you to respond with compassion — either returning the emotional weight to its rightful owner, or offering support without absorption.

You are allowed to feel with others.
But you are not required to feel for them.

You are allowed to offer presence.
But you are not required to lose yourself in another's experience.

Checking in with your emotional ownership throughout the day — gently, without judgment — helps you maintain the clarity that coherence requires.

Solitude Without Shame: Sitting With Yourself

Many people mistake solitude for failure.
In a world that often measures worth by visibility, busyness, and relational activity, being alone can feel like being forgotten, rejected, or unfinished.

But healing teaches a different relationship with solitude.
It teaches that solitude is not exile — it is presence.
It is not proof that you are unloved — it is an opportunity to become a better companion to yourself.

A note on solitude and emotional health:
Solitude can be healing when it is chosen freely and experienced as connection to yourself. But it can

also become a mask for deeper exhaustion, emotional collapse, or unaddressed pain.

If you find yourself using solitude to avoid reality — to numb with addiction, to escape responsibilities, to silence grief or fear — it is not a failure. It is a signal. A sign that you may need support, connection, or care beyond what you can provide to yourself alone.

Healthy solitude strengthens your relationship with life.
Toxic isolation slowly severs it.

The difference is not how much time you spend alone.
The difference is how you feel when you return to yourself:

- Are you growing quieter inside, but stronger?

- Or are you disappearing from yourself even when no one else is around?

You are not weak if you find yourself struggling here.
You are not failing your healing.
You are being called — gently — to reach for support that strengthens, not isolates, your coherence.

If you find that you are experiencing withdrawal, emotional collapse, or ideation, please put this book down and seek professional help or reach out to a loved one.

You have done hard work to be present in this book, and you deserve support from trained professionals who can hold space for you with skill, care, and dignity.

Learning to sit with yourself — without reaching for distraction, without scrambling to justify your quiet — is one of the most tender and transformative practices of coherence.

You do not have to love every moment of solitude. You do not have to find enlightenment in every stillness.
You only have to be willing to stay: to breathe inside your own presence without judgment, without panic, and without shame.

In solitude, you begin to hear the quieter voices inside you — the parts of yourself that do not shout to be heard because they are not trying to survive anymore.
In solitude, you begin to trust that your worth is not located in someone else's gaze or approval.

Solitude is not the absence of love.
It is the expansion of it — a love that includes yourself, even when no one else is watching.

You are allowed to be alone without being lonely.
You are allowed to sit with your own presence and find it enough.

Solitude is not a punishment for your healing.
It is one of its deepest rewards.

Joy as Alignment: Following What Brings You Alive

One of the clearest signs of healing is not just the absence of pain, but the reemergence of joy.

Joy is not a distraction from healing.
It is a companion to it — a guidepost that points you toward what strengthens your coherence, what restores your aliveness, what reminds you that life is meant to be lived, not simply endured.

After long periods of survival, joy can feel suspicious at first.
You may find yourself questioning it:

- "Do I deserve this?"

- "Am I abandoning my healing if I let myself feel good?"

- "Will this joy cost me later?"

Healing asks you to gently unlearn this suspicion.
It teaches you that joy is not a betrayal of your pain or your past.
It is the natural expression of parts of you that survived — parts of you that are ready to live, not just endure.

Following joy as a form of alignment means listening to what genuinely brings you alive — not what looks impressive, not what others expect, not what numbs you — but what feels true in your body and mind.

This could be small:

- Feeling the sun on your face during a quiet walk.

- Laughing without calculation.

- Creating something with your hands just because it feels good.

- Losing yourself in a moment of connection, art, nature, movement, or stillness.

- Witnessing your children enjoying life and not worrying about them "creating" a mess.

You do not need to chase grand, life-altering forms of happiness.
You are simply invited to notice:

Where does my breath come easier?
Where does my body feel less armored?
Where do I feel most like myself — steady, strong, and whole?

Joy, properly understood, is not indulgence.
It is coherence expressed freely, without fear.

You are allowed to seek joy without apology.
You are allowed to trust that joy is not proof that you are ignoring your healing —

It is proof that your healing is becoming part of
how you live.

Loving the Good Without Losing Yourself

Healing brings with it a complicated grace:
the ability to love what was good in the past without
losing yourself in what was harmful.

It is easy, in early healing, to fall into extremes — to
either cling to the past with desperate loyalty or to
reject it completely, erasing every memory that does
not fit the narrative of pain.
But true coherence invites something more tender,
and more honest:

*the ability to hold what was beautiful without reopening old
wounds,
and to honor your history without surrendering your future.*

You can treasure good memories without returning
to unhealthy dynamics.
You can feel gratitude for the laughter you shared,
the moments of connection, the times when love
was real — even if the relationship that once held
them cannot continue unchanged.

Loving the good does not require pretending that
the harm did not happen.
It does not require reopening yourself to cycles of
betrayal, exhaustion, or collapse.
It simply means recognizing that even inside broken
systems, love sometimes found a way to flicker —

and your ability to remember that love is a sign of your humanity, not your weakness.

Gratitude for past joy is valid.
It does not obligate you to return.
It does not obligate you to minimize your healing.

You are allowed to say:

- "This person hurt me, and there were moments of real love."

- "This place was unhealthy for me, and I still cherish parts of what I lived there."

- "This chapter is over, and I am grateful for the ways it shaped me."

Holding this complexity is a mark of emotional maturity, not confusion.

Warmth and loyalty are beautiful qualities.
They do not demand your self-abandonment to remain true.

You can carry the good forward —
treasuring it, blessing it, weaving it into who you are
—
without sacrificing the coherence you fought so hard to build.

Your healing does not erase your love.
It frees you to love more wisely, more gently, and more whole.

Objective Grace

Later, you find it again — tucked away at the back
of a drawer or a shelf you haven't visited in a while.
An object. A small thing. A relic of a different time.

At first, it brings a smile: the warmth of a memory
you thought was lost.
A day you loved.
A moment you believed would last forever.
You feel the echo of it in your body — the ease, the
laughter, the sense of being held.

And then, without warning, the weight follows:
the flood of what came after.
The betrayals.
The disillusionment.
The ache of realizing that the love was real — and
still, it was not enough to save everything.

You hold the object in your hand, caught between
tenderness and grief.
Part of you wants to throw it away.
Part of you wants to erase the confusion, the pain,
the reminder that love and hurt so often lived side
by side.

But you pause.

You breathe.

You remember:
Both feelings are true.

The beauty does not erase the harm.
The harm does not erase the beauty.

You set the object down — not in the trash; though
your first instinct was to do so, but in a place of
care.
You honor it as a witness: not of perfection, but of
your own capacity to love and to survive.

Later, you take time for yourself.
You sit quietly, perhaps with a journal, and you let
the feelings move through you.
You write what was good, what was painful, what is
yours to carry forward and what is not.

You affirm, quietly and steadily:

I cannot change what happened.
I cannot unmake the pain.
But I will not erase the good.
And I will not go back to what asked me to disappear.

You close the journal.
You breathe into your own chest, feeling the
coherence settle again — not because the past has
been rewritten, but because you have chosen to live
honestly with it.

You have not betrayed yourself.
You have not betrayed your love.
You have simply chosen to stay whole.

And this, too, is healing.

Chapter 6: Mourning and Making Room

The Hardest and Most Beautiful Work

Healing asks more of you than survival ever did. Survival taught you how to adapt, how to endure, how to shrink yourself to fit the spaces that were available. Healing, by contrast, asks you to stand still inside yourself long enough to feel what survival required you to abandon. It asks you to face the real cost of the roles you carried and the connections you preserved by betraying parts of your own truth.

This mourning is not a detour.
It is not a sign that you have failed to heal properly.
It is the most faithful act of healing you will perform:

To love what was real without pretending that it excuses what was harmful.
To grieve the versions of yourself that made belonging possible through disappearance.
To name, without erasing, both the beauty and the damage you survived.

Letting go of old patterns often feels less like liberation and more like loss, especially at first. You are not simply releasing habits; you are releasing versions of yourself — identities built to survive — and the relationships that depended on those performances. You are relinquishing the hope that love, as it was once given, could be enough if only you stayed small enough, silent enough, pleasing enough. The grief that rises in this letting go is sharp because it touches both love and loss at once.

It is tempting to try to bypass this grief, to insist that healing should feel like freedom and nothing else. But freedom, real freedom, is not numbness. It is not the absence of feeling. It is the presence of your whole truth — grief included. Mourning what you are leaving behind is not a failure of your growth. It is the acknowledgment that you mattered — even in the systems that could not see you fully — and that the cost of your survival deserves to be honored, not hidden.

You are allowed to miss what you know was never enough.
You are allowed to grieve the closeness that depended on your silence.
You are allowed to feel tenderness for the life you lived before you knew how to choose differently.

Mourning is not moving backward.
It is the slow, careful work of carrying forward only what can survive inside your coherence.
It is the hardest and most beautiful work you will do — because it requires that you hold your whole story without letting any single part of it claim ownership over who you are now.

Grieving the Loss of Old Relational Patterns

Old relational patterns are not abandoned easily, even when they have long since stopped serving you. They were built carefully, often unconsciously, through years of adapting to what was needed to stay connected, to feel valuable, to remain safe. Roles like caretaker, fixer, scapegoat, overachiever, or silent peacekeeper are not simply habits; they are survival strategies, each one born from a deep and earnest attempt to belong where belonging was conditional. When you begin to heal, you start to see these roles more clearly. You recognize the ways you bent yourself into shapes that connection required, even when those shapes left little room for your own needs, your own voice, your own truth. At first, this recognition feels empowering in the present and may even bring with it a sense of righteous anger — the fierce relief of finally seeing, perhaps for the first time, that the cost of your belonging was not invisible, and that your pain was real. Later, it often feels like mourning: the slow, aching awareness of how deeply these roles shaped your life, your relationships, and your sense of self.

A note on righteous anger:
It is natural, and often necessary, to feel anger when you first recognize how much of yourself you were

asked to give away to remain connected.
Righteous anger is not a failure of compassion.
It is the body's and heart's way of defending your
right to have existed whole all along.
This anger does not need to be rushed, buried, or
sanitized. It also doesn't require action — it requires
your ownership and to be honored by feeling it as
your own.
It deserves to be acknowledged with the same
dignity you are learning to offer your grief.
Righteous anger honors the part of you that refused,
even silently, to accept disappearance as the cost of
love.

You are not only grieving the roles themselves. You
are grieving the relationships built on top of them
— the friendships, the family dynamics, and the
intimate bonds that depended on your willingness to
disappear in small or large ways. Letting go of these
patterns sometimes means letting go of people you
love — or accepting that they will relate to you
differently, often more distantly, once you stop
offering the parts of yourself that made the
connection easy for them. It is tempting to believe
that growth should preserve all the relationships
that mattered to you, that healing should only add,
never subtract. But the reality is that not every
connection can survive your wholeness. Some
bonds were sustained not by mutual recognition,
but by the very patterns you are now learning to
release. Some love depended not just on your

presence, but on your compliance, your silence, your sacrifice — conditions that healing will no longer allow you to meet.

Grieving these losses is not a betrayal of the love you felt. It is not an indictment of the people you once cared for — and can still care for from a distance. It is simply the honest acknowledgment that the life you are building now cannot coexist with dynamics that require you to fracture yourself to belong. You may grieve intensely. You may feel waves of loneliness, anger, or guilt — wondering if you are asking too much, wondering if the gap you feel is proof that healing has left you stranded. It is not. It is proof that you are no longer willing to mistake survival for connection. The sorrow you carry is real. The ache for what was good inside what was harmful is real. The love you gave, even in broken systems, was real. But your healing asks you to grieve without returning, to mourn without undoing the boundaries that now protect your coherence.

You are allowed to miss what you know was never sustainable. You are allowed to hold gratitude and grief in the same hand, without letting either force you to forget the price you paid to stay small enough to fit. Grieving the loss of old patterns is not weakness. It is the hardest proof that your healing is real: you are willing to love yourself enough to stay whole, even at the cost of comfort, even at the cost of familiarity, even at the cost of connection that could not survive your full self.

Honoring the Love Without Clinging to Dysfunction

It is a painful truth of healing that love and harm often coexist inside the same relationships. Many of the places you learned to survive were not devoid of affection or care. There were moments when laughter felt genuine, when comfort was given freely, when love seemed real and unencumbered. These moments are not illusions, and healing does not require that you erase or devalue them. It asks for something far harder: that you learn to hold the full complexity of your experience without allowing the presence of good to invalidate the harm you endured alongside it. Love, even when sincere, is not an antidote to dysfunction. Feeling loved at times does not negate the cost you paid to remain connected when that connection demanded your self-erasure.

Healing asks you to step into a mature relationship with your memories — one where gratitude and boundaries can coexist without canceling each other out. You are allowed to honor what was good without reopening yourself to cycles that ask you to disappear. You are allowed to bless the beauty you experienced without using it as leverage against your own healing. Recognizing the real affection you were shown does not require you to deny the survival patterns that became necessary to remain close to those who could not meet you fully. It does not require you to minimize the impact of their limitations, or yours. It requires only that you refuse to let tenderness become an excuse for self-abandonment.

A note on compassion for those who wounded you:

Part of mature healing is recognizing that hurt people often hurt others — not because the harm they caused was justified, but because they were moving inside their own wounds, their own unexamined survival patterns. Understanding this does not excuse the ways you were harmed. It does not erase your grief, nor does it minimize the cost you bore. But acknowledging the brokenness in those who hurt you can make forgiveness — true forgiveness, not forced absolution — feel less like a demand and more like a natural unfolding of grief into compassion.

Forgiveness, when it comes, is not a requirement to remain close to those who injured you. Seeing their wounds clearly can soften the bitterness of the past without reopening the cycles that damaged you. You are allowed to love people through the lens of their brokenness while still refusing to resume the role their wounds once asked you to play. Compassion does not require reenactment. Love does not require collapse. Seeing others clearly is part of your healing — not an invitation to abandon it.

One of the hardest realizations in coherence is that love alone is not enough to make a relationship sustainable. No matter how real the moments of care were, no matter how strong the pull of memory or nostalgia, connection that demands your silence or compliance is not connection that can survive inside your healing. Love without respect for your full humanity is not safe. Love that depends on your fragmentation is not the kind of love you are called to rebuild, no matter how much longing or gratitude you feel for what was once good inside it. Healing does not ask you to stop loving; it asks you to stop sacrificing yourself in the name of preserving a bond that cannot hold you as whole.

Honoring the love without clinging to the dysfunction is a profound act of emotional adulthood. It requires that you resist the easy narratives that healing often tempts us to seek — the ones that would reduce people to villains or rewrite history to justify endurance. It asks you to stay present with the full weight of what you lived: that you loved, and that you were harmed, and that both are true. It calls you to live inside the tension without resolving it prematurely, to respect your own longing without using it as a weapon against your healing, and to accept that maturity means carrying complexity, not explaining it away.

You do not have to destroy your memories to protect your healing. You do not have to sever all tenderness in order to maintain your boundaries. You are allowed to carry forward the genuine care you received without re-binding yourself to relationships that demand the cost of your coherence. You are allowed to let the good memories live — cleanly, without leverage, without justification — even as you walk forward into new spaces where your love will no longer require your erasure to be accepted. Honoring the love you received is not a betrayal of your healing. It is a testament to your ability to hold reality with both hands, blessing what was beautiful without binding yourself to what cannot come with you.

Trusting That the Loneliness of Coherence Is Temporary

A note before continuing:
Not every healing journey brings deep loneliness. For some, the process of becoming more coherent deepens existing relationships or reveals new sources of support without a prolonged experience of isolation.
If you do not find yourself mourning old dynamics or feeling distanced from connection as you heal, there is nothing missing or wrong in your experience.
This chapter is here for those who encounter loneliness as part of their reorganization, but it is not a requirement or a universal stage.
If what follows feels distant from your experience, you are free to honor that — and to continue trusting the path your healing is unfolding naturally.

There is a particular loneliness that accompanies healing — a loneliness deeper and more disorienting than the familiar isolation of surviving inside broken systems. It is the loneliness that arises when you stop abandoning yourself to maintain connection, when you stop bartering pieces of your identity to secure conditional love. This loneliness is not the emptiness of being unseen by others; it is the raw awareness of standing fully in your own presence without the scaffolding of old patterns. It is the discomfort of realizing that many of the relationships you once relied on were rooted not in mutual recognition, but in mutual survival strategies, and that without those strategies, the familiar forms of belonging no longer hold.

This loneliness is not a punishment, nor is it proof that you were wrong to heal. It is the natural clearing that occurs when you stop performing for connection and allow your true needs and coherence to take up space. Healing does not immediately replace what is lost; it asks you to sit with the absence long enough for real belonging to have room to grow. The in-between space — between the survival-based relationships you are releasing and the healthier connections not yet formed — is one of the hardest parts of the journey. It can feel unbearable at times, but it is a sign of real change. It is the painful, necessary evidence that you are no longer willing to mistake proximity for intimacy, or compliance for love.

Coherence requires the willingness to endure this loneliness without rushing to fill it with more of what hurt you. It demands patience in a culture that idolizes immediacy. It asks you to trust that the ache you feel is not a warning to return to old dynamics, but an invitation to remain open long enough for something truer to emerge. Relationships that can meet you as you are — without requiring your disappearance — form slowly. They cannot be forced into existence out of fear or longing. They require the same coherence, patience, and self-respect that your healing demanded of you in solitude.

You will grieve what you have left behind. You will doubt yourself at times. You will feel the ache of old roles rising up, tempting you with the familiar comfort of shrinking to fit. But if you stay present, if you trust the space you have created, you will see that the loneliness of coherence is not permanent. It is a passage, not a life sentence. It is the difficult and necessary threshold between the world you survived and the world you are now free to build. Trust that you are not failing because you feel lonely. Trust that the new life you are cultivating is worth this temporary ache. And most importantly, trust that you are already more whole than you were when you first learned to survive.

Becoming a Home for Yourself: Creating Space for New, Aligned Relationships

Healing does not simply ask you to release unhealthy dynamics; it calls you to inhabit the space left behind with intentionality and care. When you choose to stop bending yourself to maintain connections that demanded your disappearance, you are left with a landscape that can feel both liberating and unsettling. In that clearing, the first and most lasting relationship you must tend is the one with yourself. Becoming a home for yourself is not a rejection of others, nor is it an act of isolation. It is the foundation from which future relationships can grow without requiring the old compromises that once cost you your coherence.

Learning to become a home for yourself means developing a relationship with your own needs, rhythms, and vulnerabilities that is not contingent on external validation. It means trusting that your inner life is worthy of attention even when no one else is witnessing it. In the absence of roles like caretaker, fixer, or peacekeeper, there is a quiet kind of rebuilding that must occur: the rebuilding of self-trust, of patience, of believing that your life has value beyond the functions you once performed for others. This work is not glamorous or immediately rewarding. It often feels slow, tedious, and lonely.

Yet it is in this careful tending of your own internal landscape that real stability begins to emerge.

As you cultivate a stronger relationship with yourself, the space around you becomes a place where new relationships can eventually take root. These relationships will not resemble the ones you left behind. They will not ask you to shrink, perform, or offer loyalty at the expense of truth. But they cannot be rushed into existence simply to fill the discomfort of the present. They require the same patience and discernment you have learned to extend toward yourself. Connection built from coherence grows slowly and quietly, not out of desperation but out of genuine resonance.

In this transitional space, loneliness may continue to visit you. There may be days when the emptiness feels like evidence that you have made a mistake by leaving behind familiar but harmful patterns. It is in these moments that the work of becoming a home for yourself deepens. It becomes an act of quiet defiance against the part of you that was taught to believe that survival was only possible through disappearance. Sitting with yourself through these spaces — neither abandoning your needs nor rushing to replace discomfort with familiarity — is one of the most radical acts of healing you will perform.

You are not filling your life with absence. You are cultivating the conditions for presence: first your own, and then the presence of others who can meet

you without asking you to fracture yourself.
Becoming a home for yourself is not the end of
connection. It is the beginning of a different kind of
belonging, one that does not demand self-betrayal
as its price. Trust that the loneliness you may feel
now is a passage, not a verdict. Trust that the space
you are clearing is not evidence of failure, but
preparation for a life where you can remain whole
while standing alongside others who value your
wholeness.

Chapter 7: Living Inside the Gap

Living inside the gap requires a different kind of strength than simply surviving.

It is not the strength of bracing yourself against the next impact or enduring silent losses until they become invisible.

It is the quieter, more demanding strength of choosing to remain present with yourself — fully aware of your history, your healing, and your needs — even when old survival patterns would offer easier, more familiar escape routes.

The gap you now carry is not an empty space.

It is a living environment that shapes your relationships, your choices, and your self-understanding.

It will not always feel comfortable.

There will be moments when it aches — moments when old habits call you back with the promise of simplicity, even when you know that simplicity would cost you the coherence you fought so hard to build.

You may feel, at times, a sharp loneliness where a familiar role or dynamic once filled the space.

You may wonder if healing has made you harder to reach, or if the space you now require will always feel too wide to bridge.

These doubts are not signs that you have failed.
They are signs that you are awake now.

You are no longer willing to sacrifice your wholeness for temporary comfort.
You are no longer willing to measure love by how much of yourself you must erase to receive it.

The gap reshapes how you belong to others.
Some relationships will adjust naturally within it, finding new rhythms that honor your growth.
These relationships may feel quieter, less demanding, and more deeply rooted.
Other connections will wither, unable to survive without the old emotional labor that once sustained them.
New bonds will grow more slowly, but they will be built on respect, mutuality, and genuine resonance rather than on unspoken contracts of caretaking and performance.

Living inside the gap does not mean closing your heart or isolating yourself from the world.
It means learning to love and be loved while remaining anchored to your own truth.
It means trusting your instincts when something feels out of alignment, and giving yourself permission to step back, pause, or protect your coherence — even when no one else understands why.

There will be days when the gap feels like a heavy loss.
There will be days when it feels like sacred ground — space you cleared with great courage to finally breathe, move, and grow freely.

Both experiences are true.
Both are part of carrying your healing forward.

You are not responsible for filling the gap with noise, distraction, or unearned loyalty.
You are responsible only for tending it with care — allowing it to hold space for the life you are still creating.

Living inside the gap is not a punishment for your healing.
It is the natural outcome of becoming someone who can stand in their own presence without needing to disappear.
It is the clearest proof that your life is no longer defined by survival, but by the living choice to remain coherent, even when it costs you something to do so.

Trusting Yourself Going Forward

Moving forward after healing is not a matter of arriving at a final destination. Healing does not promise a permanent end to loneliness, longing, or the temptation of old roles. It does not shield you from future pain, nor does it erase the ache of wanting simpler paths when life feels complex or unsteady. What healing offers is not the illusion of perfection. It offers the hard-won ability to remain in relationship with yourself — to notice when coherence trembles and to choose, again and again, to return to it without demanding that you or the world be free of difficulty.

Trusting yourself going forward does not mean expecting flawless navigation. You will stumble into old patterns sometimes, or pause too long in doubt, or reach for comfort in places you know can no longer sustain you. Trusting yourself means something quieter and more resilient: it means recognizing these moments not as proof of failure, but as invitations back to awareness. It means remembering that strength is not measured by never faltering, but by how gently and firmly you return to yourself when you do. Trust is built in the return, not in the absence of need for it.

You have already built something inside yourself that no one else can dismantle. You have learned to hear the early signals of misalignment: the tightening of your body when you are asked to disappear, the subtle grief that rises when you are asked to perform instead of belong, the weariness that follows abandoning yourself to earn conditional affection. You know now — not just intellectually but somatically — what it feels like to begin to leave yourself. And you know how to stop. You know how to breathe, to pause, to name your own experience before it is overtaken by others' expectations.

The life ahead of you will continue to present challenges. New relationships will test your boundaries. Old attachments will stir in ways you do not always expect. At times, the longing for the familiar will rise — the aching wish to collapse back into smaller, safer roles simply because they require less effort, less vigilance, less visible discomfort. This longing is not proof that you are failing. It is proof that you are living honestly with the tensions that coherence naturally introduces. Choosing yourself does not mean the absence of grief; it means being willing to carry the grief of growth without trading it for the anesthesia of collapse.

Healing does not promise that you will never be hurt again. It promises that when hurt comes, you will not lose yourself trying to erase it or rewrite it. You will not sacrifice your dignity in a desperate attempt to preserve relationships that cannot survive your full presence. You will not confuse suffering with loyalty. You will not confuse disappearance with love. The work you have done ensures that you can be hurt — and still remain coherent, still remain whole, still remain worthy of the life you are building.

Trusting yourself means knowing that you can endure moments of loneliness without abandoning your standards for connection. It means allowing yourself to feel sadness, confusion, anger, even despair — without using those feelings as evidence that you were wrong to heal, wrong to grow, wrong to choose yourself. It means knowing that discomfort is not a moral indictment; it is simply a natural part of living in greater alignment with your needs and your truth.

You have already proven that you can live awake. You have already proven that you can stand inside the discomfort of change without surrendering your coherence. You have already shown yourself that survival is no longer your only way of moving through the world. What lies ahead is not a test of your worth. It is an open field — one you now have the freedom, the resilience, and the dignity to walk inside with your whole self intact.

The work of healing was never to eliminate challenge. It was to equip you to meet life on your own terms: coherent, conscious, and whole. You do not need anyone else's permission to keep living in alignment with the person you have fought to become. You are not late. You are not behind. You are already walking the path you once doubted you could survive. Trust that you can keep walking it — with courage, with patience, and with all the wisdom your healing has given you.

Conclusion: Carry the Gap

Healing does not end with insight. It does not offer permanent closure, nor does it erase the ongoing work of staying coherent inside your own life. Healing invites you into a relationship with yourself that is alive and evolving, one that requires steady attention, humility, and care. It demands that you continue choosing yourself even when it would be easier to slip back into old survival strategies. It calls you to remember, day after day, that coherence is not a static state you achieve once and keep effortlessly. It is a way of living that must be tended in every new conversation, every new relationship, every new decision.

The gap you have created through healing is not a sign of failure or loss. It is not proof that you are broken or unworthy. It is the necessary space that allows your coherence to exist alongside connection, without collapse. In nature, a similar phenomenon occurs among trees. In dense forests, many trees grow close together but stop just short of touching at the highest points of their branches. This pattern is called crown shyness. It allows the trees to share the same light, the same air, the same space, without damaging one another. The gap between them is not weakness. It is a living respect for the space each tree needs to thrive without encroaching on the life of its neighbors.

Your gap serves the same purpose. It allows you to remain connected to others without losing yourself.

It preserves the breathing room your healing requires — not to create distance for the sake of distance, but to protect the integrity of the life you are still building. The gap you carry is not a wall. It is not a severance. It is the quiet, sacred breathing space that honors your wholeness and leaves room for others to meet you as you are, if they can, without asking you to disappear to maintain the bond.

The gap will not always feel comfortable. There will be moments when the ache of loneliness tempts you to close it hastily, to collapse back into familiar patterns simply to ease the discomfort. There will be moments when fear or habit convinces you that maintaining space is selfish, or unloving, or proof that you are difficult to be close to. In those moments, the work of healing deepens. Staying coherent within the gap is not an act of abandonment. It is an act of profound trust — trust that you can love without losing yourself, trust that you can belong without betraying your own needs and truths to secure acceptance.

The life ahead of you will still bring challenges. Healing does not exempt you from future difficulty or disappointment. You will encounter new relationships, new pressures, new invitations to trade your coherence for comfort. The gap will remain as a living reminder that you have a choice now — a space between reaction and response, between fear and freedom, between collapse and staying whole. It will not always be easy to honor the gap. But each time you do, you reinforce the life you have fought to reclaim: a life rooted in coherence rather than survival.

Healing was never about eliminating difficulty. It was about equipping you to meet life's inevitable struggles with steadiness, compassion, and clarity. It was about teaching you to remain present to yourself — to walk forward with your whole self intact, even when the path is uncertain or the ache of longing rises up to call you back into old roles.

You are not leaving your healing behind when you step into the future. You are carrying it with you — quietly, bravely, and whole. The gap is not your exile. It is your inheritance. It is the breathing space that protects your life, your love, and your truth.
Carry it with care.
Carry it with pride.
Carry it all the way home.